Pete

**the complete
byron the
penguin**

ISBN: 978-1-4710-8125-5

1 2 5 1 7 5 2 5

Front cover: Byron Penguin looking North

Penguin Philosophy

Byron the Penguin

The Imperial Rhyme

The Trial of Byron the Penguin

Byron the Penguin's Adventure

Byron in Space

**Byron the Penguin's New Year
Revolution**

**Byron Returns (The Return of Byron
Penguin)**

Penguin Philosophy

A penguin gazed across the sea

Thinking philosophic –lee

He'd argued with his good friend Buster

Of Nietzsche's Thus Spake Zarathrusta

Of getting stuck on page thirteen

Because his tiny brain was hurtin'

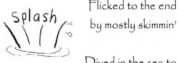

Flicked to the end
by mostly skimmin'

Dived in the sea to
do some swimmin'

Byron the Penguin

Byron Penguin stood alone

Life was just a joke

There was nothing on the telly

And the DVD was broke

"It's no good standing here" he thought

"I could be here all week,

With snow amongst my feathers

And ice upon my beak"

"Perhaps I'll dive in for a swim

And then, perhaps, I mightn't

There's sharks and
whales and leopard seals

And they might make me
frightened"

He gazed across the southern sea

And ruffled up a feather

Then went inside to have his tea

And wait for better weather

The Imperial Rhyme

Byron Penguin's head poked out

The weather was much better

Then up popped
Postman Penguin

Handing him a
letter

'Twas a summons from the Emperor

For a new Imperial Rhyme

He was fed up with the old one

As he'd had it for some time

He'd given Byron seven days

To honour his request

And promised him a medal

To wear upon his chest

Byron had to write the
poem

As famous poets do

Then recite in front of
royalty

And other penguins too

He'd have to have his feathers preened

And at the same appointment

Polish up his pointed beak

With Special Penguin Ointment

But first of all, of course

There had to be a poem

So Byron donned his thinking cap

Determined he would show 'em

But Byron couldn't get a rhyme

So thought he'd try a sonnet

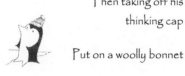

Then taking off his
thinking cap

Put on a woolly bonnet

Byron struggled on for days

The rhyme it wouldn't come

His furrowed brow grew deeper

He looked extremely glum

Then, like a flash
of lightning

The rhyme came –
heaven sent

Byron Penguin's Imperial Rhyme –

And this is how it went:

"Great Ruler of the Penguins

So Fearless, Fine and Bold

How come, with all your power

My feet are always cold?"

Well, the Emperor was most amused

He hadn't laughed so much in ages

His servants got a holiday

And he doubled up their wages

As for Byron Penguin,

There was no medal in a box

Instead the Emperor
gave to him

A pair of knitted socks

The Trial of Byron the Penguin

All along the icecap, a wave of
disbelief

Byron the Penguin slapped in
jail like a common thief

The Emperor Penguin's
favourite bard

Chief Rhymester of the Reign

Arrested by the palace guard

Forced to wear
the ball and chain

The bard was charged with
plagiarising

(Copying, to you and me)

They had computers analysing

His reams of poetry

They found repeated words and
rhymes

So they called Byron a villain

For borrowing some famous lines

From Wordsworth and Bob
Dylan

Accused of stealing someone's
rhymes

Our perfect
cavaliero

Some would stoop to these low
crimes

But surely not our hero?

Anyhow, he went to court

To tell it how it is

But Byron stood in silent
thought

Like in some kind of dizz

It became an inquisition

A great extravaganza

When the poet took up his
position

And just refused to answer

They quizzed
him low, they quizzed him
high

Did so
interrogate

But none could chisel one reply

From the silent laureate

They showed exhibits A to Y

Extracts: first to fifty third

Every single one a lie

Byron never spoke a word

So stars of
stage and screen and
sport

Vouched for
him – Soccer Penguin Totti

Came, and De Niro Penguin
stood in court

As well as Penguin Pavarotti

Who waddled slowly like a clown

Paused to take his slimming pill

Sang Byron's praises then
bowed down

Like a golden
daffodil

The judge
weighed all the evidence

Spoke with first class elocution

About the weight of the defence

And six tons of prosecution

He placed the weights upon the
scales

Of justice, adjusted with
precision

Exactly so it rarely fails

To give the wrong decision

The judge summed up and in his
speech

Advised such poetry

Was to be taken out of reach

Of civilised society

One thing could save our
Byron's day

- An Imperial Proviso

But the emperor was far away

Someplace outside Valparaiso

So the judge faced Byron in the dock

Showing no repentance

At five to ten on
the courtroom clock

Gave out a sim'lar
sentence

No cloud no relique of the
sunken day

Caught the mood when the
judge did speak

The public gallery shouted "Nay"

Byron raised his pointed beak

So Byron sits in his ten foot cell

Not gazing at the bars

Like Oscar Wilde, he's
feeling swell

And looking at the stars

Byron the Penguin's Adventure

The penguins signed a
Grand Petition

To free Byron
Penguin from his prison

An airplane took Penguin De Niro

Via Rio De Janeiro

To meet the emperor on vacation

Who'd changed his holiday location

From Valparaiso to Venezuela

But De Niro returned an empty failure

Byron couldn't even apply for bail

So he wrote The Ballad of Penguin Jail,

Page after page (got writer's cramp)

But couldn't post it off without a stamp

Frustrated, angry, feeling cross

Asked to see the prison boss

They gave him
appointment Friday week

The bard just snapped
that pointed beak

At last the day came for his meeting

Guvnor gave a cordial greeting

But said free postage stamps was agin the
rules

The guvnor said We're not a bunch of
fools

Writing poems isn't work

And nary a jailbird's allowed to shirk

So Byron (with a trusty mentor)

Went down the prison job centre

For work to suit a famous rhymer

Asked for a job as a part timer

Perhaps prison librarian?

Or better- work in the aquarium

The perfect job, a penguin's wish

Warm surroundings, lots of fish

No way, they said, they're in your care

And eating them just isn't fair

Ok says Byron at all the clucking

Just the odd one when no-one's looking

So the bard began
his new career

Making sure the
water's pure and clear

Feeding them a balanced diet

And eating small ones on the quiet

A mistake was made with the piranhas

He dipped his beak they went bananas

The doctor bandaged up his beak

Put him off fish for a whole week

Next time he dipped he used a net

Not being ready to die just yet

Settled down to his old routine

Rainbow fish and the odd sardine

One morn thought that he'd been caught

Sent to guvnor's office on report

While waiting in the outer office

Begin admiring guvnor's fish

Swimming helpless in a bowl

Byron took pity on the soul

Dipped his head to take a look

Got the goldfish bowl stuck

Drunk the water to liberate

The fish which he then ate

Our bard panicked at the
guvnor's tread

Caught with fish bowl on his head

But the guvnor said "What have we here?

Is this a spaceman volunteer?"

Byron, like he does, stayed schtum

(World champion at playing dumb)

Found out the guvnor's little scam

Sending jail birds to the space program

No penguin with any sense to spare

Would ever dream of going there

It was dangerous and underpaid

And difficult to make the grade

So prisoners were offered full parole

If they enlisted for the role

The bard, insane (as well as mental)

Thought it a bit experimental

But seeing as how freedom beckoned

Didn't waste a single second

Countersigned upon the
docket

Joined up to ride the rocket

Shipped him off to spacecraft school

To study astrophysics, rocket fuel

And obligatory extra courses

To learn about them weird g-forces

Soon he'd learnt all they had taught

Became the only Penguin Astronaut

No-one else but the bard

Had passed; the work was
far too hard

So at his solo graduation

Byron thought he'd get a grand ovation

But they just laughed at his expense

At this lunatic that had no sense

And Byron realised why they laughed

When he was introduced to his spacecraft

A rusted scrapyard kind of mix

Built in 1956

With CCCP etched on the side

Byron blinked and could have died

No way is that for me he spoke

That rocket is a cruel joke

But shown the small print on the
docket

Byron had to climb inside the rocket

For refusal classified as "Fail"

And meant going straight to jail

No passing go, no two hundred pounds

It's back to chokey with no grounds

So reluctantly, our bard inside

Spacesuit on and petrified

Byron held a letter with his mission

A mechanic started the ignition

The engine coughed and groaned and
then

It started, someone counted down from ten

Ten to one goes pretty fast

Soon Byron shot off in a blast

Somewhere in the atmosphere

The crowd gave an ironic cheer

Byron flying high, feeling better

Had a shufty at his letter

Told him to gather information

On a major threat to penguin nation

Namely why was the icecap shrinking?

So Byron did a bit of thinking

Switched on the music player

And spun around the ozone layer

Rocket Man on the earphone

He spied a hole in the old ozone

Twisted round, cricked his neck

In his earhole the theme from Star Trek

Tried to steer while Sinatra crooned

The classic Fly Me To the Moon

Typical just trying to have a look

Got the stupid rocket stuck

And news came from mission control

That Byron had bunged up the hole

Had stopped the air evaporating

Found a committee nominating

Byron for an Imperial prize

A sum of considerable size

Which Byron couldn't claim with grace

Since he was partly in and out of space

This suited Penguin Chief of Treasure

Gave him quite enormous pleasure

Kept the cash and still looked good

The reverse of Robin Hood

And Byron waiting for the rescue

Until they trained a second crew

Which could take months or even years

Because they couldn't get no volunteers

So if you want to be an astronaut

Don't give it another thought

You might get chance to save the earth

But first ask Byron what it's worth

To be miles above where you belong

Playing tapes and singing along

You might be better off as you are

Than to be swinging on a star

Byron in Space

 Byron our heroic soul

Had saved the earth, don't doubt it

His rocket plugged the ozone hole

He wrote a rhyme about it

The emperor, glad to be alive

Had sent a bunch of plaudits

And a rescue craft, due to arrive

As soon as he could afford it

Now Byron Penguin wasn't daft

He'd seen the Emperor Penguin's wad

So if he couldn't afford a rescue craft

He would have to send a pod

A capsule maybe would be sweet

Byron hummed a little tune

Relaxed and angled back his
                          seat

For a nice view of the moon

Days went by, turned into weeks

In fact the entire summer

The hole got bigger, forming leaks

And Byron was no plumber

Supplies were down, electrics blew

He used the special cranking handle

To radio through to Space
HQ

To send matches and a candle

But Byron was unaware

The staff was on vacation

There wasn't anybody there

To receive communication

The bard called again
loud and clear

Not a touch of static

Thought they'd all turned a deaf ear

His behaviour turned erratic

Byron, mad, shot flares at Mars

Erupted in hysteric

On earth they looked like shooting stars

Very atmospheric

The bard set off a
few maroons

Tried to change the pattern

Folks thought they were exploding moons

On the other side of Saturn

The bard was ailing, feeling weak

Miserable and rotten

Downcast that once
defiant beak

How could he be
forgotten?

So on his own he had to try

To get his craft unstuck

Rear fins were bent, but they would fly

Got out to take a look

He took a walk around
the front

With a jemmy and a
crowbar

Ozone was tough – the jemmy blunt

What he needed was a tow bar

And a Samaritan to pull him free

(A miracle or two)

When lo, what did Byron see?

Redemption – out the blue

Cruising on the wind of fates

The Penguin Plumber Band

Leaks fixed at the going rates

All jobs cash in hand

They came to take a closer look

At the bard's calamity

Agreed to get the craft unstuck

For a quite enormous fee

Two minutes and a job
well done

Cash exchanging pockets

Both parties free to chase the sun

In their respective rockets

One problem solved, but great dismay

The earth was back in danger

For the atmosphere just slipped away

Through the hole of the climate changer

Byron said "Hold on my friends

Do you fix holes in ozone layers"

The chief said "It all depends

On how much you want to pay us"

Byron said. "I thought you might,

Like, do the job for free

Save the earth from an awful plight

Altruist-ic-ally"

The chief laughed at Byron's joke

Laughed heartily, laughed thrice

Almost began to choke

When Byron asked for it cost price

"I'll do a deal," chief tied his shoe

Quoth quids to build a lattice

"That's the best that I can do"

Threw in the parts for gratis

"The materials will come for free?"

Said Byron. "Oh yes, straight off the shelf"

The bard said "Leave it all to me

I'll do the job myself"

So now who laughed at Byron's joke

As the chief gave away some plastic

Sour-faced said "Don't tell other folk"

Threw in a tub of mastic

Now came 'pon that Byronic Beak

A burnished bright defiance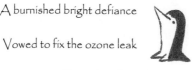

Vowed to fix the ozone leak

(It was hardly rocket science)

The plumbers laughed and called him
names

As he did the installation

But soon they forgot their games

Looked on in admiration

The job complete the planet safe

Let every penguin know it

Let no emperor or simple waif

Underestimate a poet

Byron the Penguin's New Year Revolution

Restless penguins
marched upon

The emperor's winter quarters

They swam across the Rubicon

- Byron's true supporters

The Emperor had made a pledge

To bring Byron Penguin home

The bard was drifting to the edge

Of space and all alone

He'd found and fixed the ozone leak

And saved the earth below

And now he wished to bring his beak

To fish in ice and snow

Byron's friends besieged The Court

They were running out of verse

Times were hard and sonnets short

The rhymes were getting worse

They came up to the battlement

Gathered by the moat

Emperor refused a settlement

Scared that next
they'd want the vote

Instead he read an Act Of State

Said bard's licence had expired

And so the Poet Laureate

Had been summarily fired

This act was mean and ill advised

The crowd became a throng

But tyrants seldom realise

When they've done something wrong

The Emperor wouldn't help their plight

Didn't understand their loss

Promised them a snowball fight

To show them he was boss

He froze Byron's bank account

In an Imperial Fit Of Pique

No worries – by a small amount

The bard was overdrawn that week

Outside the castle's icy walls

The penguin throng did riot

And a fusillade of snowballs

Failed to keep them quiet

The battlements were overrun

By revolutionary hordes

Who fought with neither blade nor gun

But beaks as sharp as swords

The Emperor was packing cash

And his pet canaries

Knowing that he'd have to dash

Off to Buenos Aires

The Empress, well, she saved his skin

No-one could've stopped her

Bundled him and his suitcase in

The Imperial Helicopter

The revolution – short but grim

Done within the hour

They needed someone- "Interim"

To assume the threads of power

Who could become the head of state?

Take penguin under wing?

Reinstate the Laureate?

It had to be a Penguin King

King Penguin, he was duly found

Religiously anointed

Beneath the Southern Cross was
crowned

(Kings couldn't be
appointed)

The King's first act was very wise

To get folks in his pocket

A rescue craft was authorised

To find Byron Penguin's rocket

Byron (still ex laureate)

But assets now unfrozen

Prepared himself for a long wait

Whilst the rescue team was chosen

The King then pulled a master stroke

A title so prestigious

That Byron thought it was a joke

To be named Versificator Regis

As for Byron's right to rhyme

The King to Byron wrote

"Pay me when you've got the time

- Enclosed: one cover note"

And so The Cause of the Revolt

Soon paid his two and fi'pence

For every poet worth his salt

Needs some poetic licence

Byron Returns (The Return of Byron Penguin)

Byron faced another day, rubbed sleep
out of his eye

Stretched his wings as if to say "If only I
could fly"

He was stuck in outer space, Sector Nine
but didn't know it

Could have been in any place, one poor
discarded poet

Abandoned by his penguin chums, Byron
in a fix

Sat and twiddled penguin thumbs,
composing limericks

Waiting for salvation out in the Great
Unknown

The poet's expectation was to fade away
alone

Byron tried to write an ode, the
sun glanced off his beak

Sent an SOS in code, he was fading
fast and weak

Call it destiny or horoscope the signal
found its way

Appeared upon a telescope out on the
Milky Way

Across the starry gridline a miracle
occurred

Ghost rider sent to Sector Nine to save
the stricken bird

Unless the rider found the mite things
were looking grim

Hours passed at speed
of light and then it
spotted him

Byron spied the riding ghost, a penguin
one of course

It was the thing he wanted most to ride a
winged white horse

Byron weakly said "How do" to masked
and ghostly stranger

"Have you come to my rescue like a
Space Lone Ranger?"

"Well yes" said the ghosted thing "Since
you care to ask

Jump up on my steed with wings" and
adjusted his black mask

But Byron was a clever bard: could this
ghost be trusted?

He asked to see his ID card to prove he'd
cut the mustard

"I don't have identity, I am Ghost Without
A Name

I'm just a roving entity and my horse has
got no mane"

Byron was alone and lost
he didn't have much choice

"Pray tell how much this ride will cost" he
asked in his small voice

"This ride can only once be sold by ghost
upon patrol

The journey costs to penguin bold, the
small price of your soul"

Byron didn't really feel that he could go
that far

And so the ghost - to seal the deal threw
in lessons on guitar

The poet moved this way and that then he
hummed and hawed

The ghost gave him a Fender Strat and
Byron strummed a chord

Now Byron hadn't played before, amazed
to find that soon

Could play as well as Dave Gilmour on
Dark Side Of The Moon

The ghost was truly on a roll, had proved
his dark credentials

So Byron said "I'll sell my soul, but keep it
confidential"

"Another thing that troubles me - is how
far can you go?"

"Further than infinity and then a mile or so"

Byron thought that quite a lot, but
dithered to decide

The ghost said "Are you on or not?"
Byron jumped on for the ride

They rode across the heaven, course
marked for Byron's sea

Via Sector Seven but stopping twice for
tea

They came upon the earth by night, a haze
of blue and green

Except for Byron's patch of white where
beauty could be seen

They entered upper atmosphere and
Byron set his beak

He shed a small homecoming tear, it rolled
across his cheek

The ghost wrapped himself around, saved
Byron's feathers burning

Soon they were almost on the ground, the
poet was returning!

Byron landed on the ice, slid across the
snow

To be at home felt very nice, inside he felt
aglow

The penguins welcomed him and how!
Their poet superstar

B.B. Penguin (renamed for now), playing
blues guitar

What happened to the Riding Ghost?
With Byron's soul he vanished

And Byron fished along the coast 'cause
he was flippin' famished

By Appointment
Versificator Regis

16411406R00044

Printed in Great Britain
by Amazon